Abduction Etiquette

Jim Ryan
MONOLOGUES

Main Street Rag Publishing Company
Charlotte, North Carolina

Copyright © 2011 Jim Ryan

Cover art courtesy of iStockPhoto.com

Author photo: Eric Coates

Acknowledgments:

livejournal.com: "Sleep!"
The Main Street Rag: "Death & Taxes,"
   "Kingdom of Java"

Library of Congress Control Number: 2011935278

ISBN: 9781599483061

Produced in the United States of America

Main Street Rag
PO Box 690100
Charlotte, NC 28227
www.MainStreetRag.com

This work is dedicated to the owners and denizens of Ibby's Coffee House, Nocturna, the Algonquin Coffee House, the Living Room and every other establishment where I've been allowed to act silly in public. Without those places, these monologues would never have existed.

It is also dedicated to the memory of Innis A. Ryan, a wonderful actress whom I think would have enjoyed reading it, and who did me the very good turn of giving birth to me.

CONTENTS

ACT I

Kingdom of Java. 3
Death & Taxes. .5
Disgruntled Postal Worker 6
Leprechaun Psychology 8
Beelzebub's Bar & Grill 10
Psychological Carnival 11
Penguin Death From on High 12
Zombie Aid 13
Ballad of the Highwayman 14
Unhappy Trees 16
Mouse Driver 18
Philosopher's Dateline 19
Violence 20
Karmic Garbage 22
Pet Project 23
The Car Of The Future 25
Extermination Through Understanding. 27
Abduction Etiquette 29

ACT II

Shakespeare Relay 33
Secret Horoscope 35
Sleep! 36
Doc's Steakhouse 37
The Vampire Chickens! 39
Cromagnon Mechanic 40
Elk Attack 41

Open Mic Torture 43
Forecasting Made Easy 44
Dragon-on-a-Stick 45
Chernobyl Resort 46
Pittsburgh vs Cleveland Beyond the Grave 48
Thanksgiving Report. 50
Canadian Mongoose 51
Apocalyptic Runway Models 53
Dream Director 55
Horns of Vengeance 57
Funeral Pyre 58

ACT III

Mad Appliance 62
Return to Sender. 63
Answering Machine 65
Tour of Hell. 67
Crossword Gremlins 69
Peanut Huntin' 70
Smoking Clothes 71
Monster's Perspective 72
Wookie Love 73
Cruise Control 74
Fish Condoms. 76
Forensics 101 78
Phone Sex 79
Auto Racing Spectator 80
Voodoo Clinic 81
Paranormal Insurance 82
Anti-Talk Show 83
This Is The End 85

ACT I

KINGDOM OF JAVA

Welcome, friends, to the Holy Caffeinate. I am Archbishop Oral, and I can be your guide to the everlasting Kingdom of Java if you believe in the healing power of caffeine. Friends, the path to inner enlightenment through the grinding and consumption of the glorious coffee bean is often marred with pitfalls of indecision. Many pretenders come up to us every day with promises of a better life through their mochas and espressos. But, the truth of the matter is that it makes no difference how you take it. All that matters is that you allow the righteous rush of the substance to enter your veins, and you will feel the power of it come upon you and carry you into a land of heightened awareness of unparalleled proportions: the ultimate adrenal ecstasy! But sometimes it's not so easy, friends. Sometimes Satan, in all of his twisted trickery, will make it more difficult for you to have your caffeine in the morning. He may sneak into your kitchen at night and put your coffee somewhere you can't find it, or take the last of it for himself, leaving you to cast false blame on your loving spouse when morning comes. Or sometimes, he will titillate you with whispered lies about his own dark invention, the dreaded "Decaf!" You see, friends, Satan knows that if you begin to partake of the one true caffeine, you will be more awake, aware, alert and able to find him out more easily. So he broadcasts his lying television commercials with people getting up in the morning, drinking his accursed Decaf and somehow, by some unnatural and unholy ritual, being woken up by it and given the energy to face the day. But don't be fooled by it, friends! Those actors are filled with Satan's dark, drug-enhanced energy! He wants to turn this world into a shrunken, decaffeinated, bleary-eyed land of groaning misfits thumping around in the dark and never getting out of bed until 2 PM! But you can change all that. Satan is like that old, hardened, blackened coffee bean that just won't come out right. But you've got to grab him by his tough shell and grind him up in the Cuisinart of Redemption, pour the Scalding Water of Salvation all over him and strain him through the Filter of Righteousness! Friends, for a small contribution, we will send you our thanks and prayers and help you to pick up that old and cracked coffee pot of truth and pour yourself a cup of enlightenment! The number is on your screen. Now, let us pause for a moment of prayer, reflection, and an important message from Sanka.

DEATH & TAXES!

Good evening and welcome to Death & Taxes! Today's contestants will be competing to see who gets the biggest tax break and who gets to live longest! Here, briefly, is how the game works. Each contestant itemizes his W-2 and then proceeds to fill out his 1099. If he has any dependants to declare, he must also fill out the 1170. If he declares the wrong number of dependants, the man-eating tiger will be released into his cell. If a contestant has any deductibles, he refers to the 1027. If he has any questions about the 1027, he only need refer to Schedule A on the 1590. If he finds his 1099 inadequate in any other way, he then will have 30 seconds to correlate his 1750, 1170, 1820 and 1560 with his J-7, W-2, 1320 and 1984. And from there, we move on to the bonus round. For every correct answer, the contestant receives enough bread and water for one more day. For every incorrect answer, he'll be penalized one limb. If at any point a contestant submits a form without copying it first or if he is unable to complete his forms in the allotted time, the man-eating tiger will be released into his cell. And at the end of the game, the last surviving contestant gets to come back tomorrow and do it all over again to defend his title as returning champion. Do we all understand the rules? Great! Then let's play Death & Taxes!

DISGRUNTLED POSTAL WORKER

Hello. My name's Bud and I represent your friendly local post office. I'm just one of the many hard workers who do our damnedest to make your life better. I get up at 4:30 every morning, put on my bright blue uniform, and go out to join my fellow postal workers in their task. Of course, it's not easy. No sir. We've got millions of letters coming in every day. And we've got to process each and every one of those letters. At 5 in the morning. Now, granted, we're not perfect, believe it or not. And every now and then, a few letters will slip through the cracks and get misplaced or dead-ended. But, that's not our fault! Sometimes, some of you nice customers of ours will make a mistake or two. You know, like forgetting to put down a return address, which is why we have labels for that now. Or you'll forget to put stamps on your envelopes, just assuming we'll deliver them for free, I guess. Or sometimes, you don't even put an address on your mail—not sure why—that really defeats the purpose of sending the damn thing in the first place. And then, you come to US when your mail doesn't show up on time, or it's been damaged or opened. Well, how the hell else do you expect us to know where the goddamn things are supposed to go when you're screwing them up all the time before we even get them?! Hell, I can't read your tiny, spidery handwriting anyway, you stupid jerks! Don't you realize that we're doing all we can to protect you from yourselves?!! Without us, society would totally collapse, and the world would be a stinking, craterous hellhole! But what do you care? You all have E-mail now. You're all a bunch of pinko commie subversives who only care about themselves and don't give a damn about the honest, hard-working postal carriers that keep all of your asses alive! Hell, you deserve to die! You should all be lined up and shot like the cowering bastards that you are! Heck, why don't I just do it right now, and put you all out of your misery? It's not like I've got crap to live for. Sure, why the hell not?! That's it! Your numbers are all up! You can't escape us. We're the post office. We know where you live! Where's my uzi?!!!

LEPRECHAUN PSYCHOLOGY

[INSERT IRISH BROGUE HERE]

Now sir, let's get on to our last topic. You say you've been seeing... little people? Could you describe them to me? Green coats and little top hats? Ah. When do you usually see them? At times of stress, perhaps? Not particularly? I see. What exactly do these little people do? Ah, yes. Drinking, dancing, playing the violin? Hmm... Have you been drinking a lot lately? Ah, no, I see sir. I try to stay off the ol' spirits as often as I can, as well. I wish I had your resolve. So when did you first start seeing them? That's about when you came into your fortune, isn't it? Hmm... So, what happened? Ah. You caught one, did you? `Tis a major hallucination indeed, sir, I must say. Well, little people with green coats? Really, sir. Ah... no sir. You needn't raise your voice. Just breathe. Perhaps you're harboring some kind of resentment. What else happened? He played games with you. What do you mean, sir? Teleporting from place to place? Hiding? Running away? Well, you probably terrified the poor fella. That is to say, sir, you terrified the image of him you had in your mind. That's what I meant. Yes. Why do you seem so resentful? What did this little fella do to you? He made you wear... a pair of green shoes? Well, that's silly. We haven't used the green shoes in years. Er, no sir, just speculating about something. Made you dance around, did he? Well, what did you do to him to make this figment of your imagination so upset? You did what?! Put him in a cage? Now, whatever would make you do a daft thing like that? Oh, I see, sir. You got the idea into your head that he was a leprechaun and you held him against his will when he wouldn't lead you to his pot of gold! You know, I've got a lot of patients like you who keep thinking that they're seeing the little people. You're all the same! You keep hunting them down, trapping them, forcing them to give you all they own, demanding to be taken to the end of the rainbow. I mean, really. What self-respecting leprechaun would hide his gold in such an obvious place? But you never let up, do you? What do you think we are, made of money?! **(pause)** Sorry, sir... no, it was nothing. Just a bit of role-playing to see how you'd react. Very good. I think, sir, that these little people are all in your head. They're phantoms brought on by a guilt complex you've developed from stumbling across that pot of gold you mentioned finding that one day that brought you your fortune, and you created these leprechauns as a way of justifying your amazing luck. Well, I see that we're out of time. Just give your check to Mr. Darby out in the waiting room, as usual. I'm sure that after a few more sessions, we'll have you as good as new. Good day, sir! **(pause) (under his breath)** Faith and begorrah, there must be an easier way to get our money back than this!

BEELZEBUB'S BAR & GRILL

Are you a doomed soul who's tired of the ordinary grind of unbearable damnation or just a poor, masochistic bastard who hungers for more? Then come by Beelzebub's Bar & Grill, voted the most horrific establishment throughout the Inferno. Come out and sample the flesh kabobs, play demonic darts or while away the centuries as a host of sinful bands wail in terror without a single break between sets. Come and listen to the millions of soul-crushing tunes on the giant Juke Box of Torture or play an exhilarating round of nine ball on the Pool Table of Despair; finally, you get to BE the ball! Stop by the bar and Beelzebub's grandson will mix you up a horrifying chaser. Throw back our famous, fear-inspiring gin and tonic. Our Extra-Bloody Mary lets you taste the evisceration. Or enjoy the unending pain of our Bourbon Fireball—get perpetually smashed with shot after shot of unbearable anguish! If you're feeling hungry, or just up for a bit of gluttony, try our hellfire-baked pretzels. Just cry out and our hellish cooks will fire up the open pit and toss some demon wings on the barbecue pyre. We've got sandwiches that'll stick to your ribs for eternity! And afterward you can sit back and watch as our impish dancers trample a swath of destruction across the floorboards to music played by the Most Evil DJ in the Universe. If you're on a hard-core self-destructive binge, every Ladies' Night there's free emasculation until midnight! And there are always gruesome prizes to be won in our nightly vivisection contest. If you've been cursed to suffer the flames of everlasting damnation but STILL can't get enough, come and get the visceral agony you deserve at Beelzebub's Bar & Grill. Located on the 9th Ring of Hell, over by Dante's Hockey Rink. Unhappy Hour 5-7 nightly.

THE PSYCHOLOGICAL CARNIVAL

Hurry, hurry, hurry! Come to the Psychological Carnival and see the wonders of the inner mind. Come and ride the emotional rollercoaster! Feel every bump of life's ups and downs! Feel the thrill of a raging bipolar disorder with a ride on the mood swings. Come to the Head Games Gallery and try your skill at the Rorschach Test. Take a tour through the Hall of Disillusionment. Or take a ride through the kleptomaniac's haunted house: room after room of nothing but white walls. Also helps those with attention deficit disorder. Come and sit in the agoraphobic booths: your own personal closet space! Come and visit the freak show, with some of the world's strangest oddities. See the Sensitive Guy, the Antisocial Lady, the Turrets Oratorio and the Epileptic Ballet. Ride the Great Depression! Schizophrenics can visit the Hall of Mirrors and talk to themselves for hours on end! Bring your imaginary friends! Or you ladies can stop by the gift shop and have your picture taken wearing a Freudian Slip. Get your tickets right here! It's fun for the whole dysfunctional family!

PENGUIN DEATH FROM ON HIGH

Repent! Repent my brethren, for the end of the world is nigh! You feel that we are safe, but we are mere steps away from oblivion! The agents of evil are already among us. I speak, of course, of those most wretched of the avians—the fearful and dreaded penguins! These dark birds of the apocalypse shall descend upon us as we lay sleeping and devour the Earth! Do not be fooled by their comical waddling and amusing countenances, for they mean to crush us all beneath their clawed feet and snap the seventh seal in their mighty beaks. They have already begun to infiltrate our ranks. At first they present themselves in documentaries as lovable creatures, seeming nowhere near the demonic fowls that they truly are. Then they appear in public zoos where we are brainwashed and made to be their slaves and minions, bringing them food and giving them a comfortable environment. Soon they shall be entering our very homes in the guises of friendly and lovable pets. And it is then, my brethren, that the penguins shall strike! Their sharp beaks are the scythes that shall mow the human race like a harvest, and their severely colored feathers are the very dress suits we shall be wearing when we are carried to our graves. So do not give in to them, my brethren! Do not be commanded by their powerful gaze. Pay them no heed when the penguins come to you in the night, squawking outside your window. Do not be swayed when they visit you in your dreams and whisper to you of unbridled power beyond your imagination. You must be steadfast in this time of crisis as the penguins begin their plans to coat the planet in ice with their megalithic freezing ray. Pray for your souls, my brethren, for the penguins are coming! Pray, repent and try to keep warm!

ZOMBIE AID

The undead have it pretty bad, you know. They rise from their graves every night with barely enough energy to shamble about and terrorize the populace. Many of these zombies are so run down that they're almost unable to walk the streets. Most must be resigned to a fate of wandering aimlessly until they no longer have the energy to even walk, let alone disembowel someone. Slowly, these poor, misunderstood walking cadavers are dying... again. Just look at these destitute zombies. Their sad, gaping mouths are so decayed from lack of fresh brains that they can hardly speak. Their eyes are so sunken and hollow they can't even cry on their coffin's pillows when they rest. But you can help. For just fifteen cents a day, you can sponsor one of these unfortunate walking dead and provide him with the human flesh he needs to continue his rampage. You'll receive a picture of the harrowed unfortunate that you sponsor tearing someone limb from limb, along with his case history and death certificate. You can even write letters to your zombie. He won't be able to read them, but it'll make a nice gesture, anyway. You can turn the existence of these poor members of the mortally challenged community around. So call now to help a disheartened, animate corpse find new life again... and eat it.

BALLAD OF THE HIGHWAYMAN

Roll up and see the mechanical bird.
Come here and listen to its every word.
A wonder of wonders, it chirps out your name,
You've just got to listen, I'm sure you'll be game.
Just amble on over and put down some cash.
I promise you'll love it; please stay, don't be rash.

No?

Do you like hearing the holy church bells?
Perhaps you will listen to this magic shell.
A chorus of angels is hidden inside.
Their voices are lovely and chiming with pride.
Just hoof it on over and pay a small fee.
I promise its music will fill you with glee.

No?

Have you a soul that is tender and mild?
Perhaps you will listen to this starving child.
This poor lad's so hungry, he's stiff as a board.
He's not carved from logs, he just looks it, milord.
Just wander on over and do him some good.
I promise he just looks to be made of wood.

No?

Then, just one more item before we're all done.
Perhaps you will listen to my trusty gun.
Hand over your money, before I'm enraged.
I gave a performance, now time for my wage.

Abduction Etiquette

Just saunter on over and hand me your purse.
And let's have a smile, for it could be much worse.

Yes? Ah…

I see now that you're the most clever of men.
And though I'm a fraud, I must bow to your ken.
I'll now take my leave, and your money as well.
No need to be flustered, I swear I'll not tell.
I must say, you've been in the finest of humors
And, if I may say, a most gracious consumer.

UNHAPPY TREES

Welcome, friends. I'm glad you could join me again. Today, we'll be doing a simple forest scene. You can start with some Forest Green mixed in with just a touch of Cadmium Yellow to give it a kind of "autumny" feel. Let's make some little bushes just around here. It's very important to make sure your bushes don't get too big, or they start trying to take over and then you have to go in with the hedge clippers and teach them a lesson… heh heh…. Now we can get out the knife and put something there in between these bushes. Let's make a bridge with just a smattering of Burnt Umber. Just a little footbridge, now. Nothing too complicated. The smaller the bridge, the easier it is to take down when you have to defend yourself from invaders. Just a touch, there. Now, let's get our brushes out again and start making some tall, leafy trees. You always want to make sure your trees are happy trees… 'cause you never know. Your trees might all **look** happy, but if one subversive dogwood or larch sneaks in it can sow discontent among its neighbors and before you know it, the whole forest is against you. So you've got to know what to look for. Look at this tree, for example. It looks like a happy tree, but if you look closely you can see a self-satisfying smirk on its little tree face. That pine is definitely up to something. See? You see it whispering lies to all the other trees? They look like they're planning something. Can't you see them staring out at us hungrily with their beady little eyes as they ready their attack on the village? See, their roots are already moving up to the bridge. They're going to take the bridge! We've got hostile trees at 2 o'clock! Fall back! Oh my god, they're coming over the wall! Where's the air support? Drop the Agent Orange! Get more Cadmium Yellow out there now! That's an order, mister! We've never lost a painting before and we sure as hell aren't going to lose one on my watch! Blow the bridge! Blow it! **(pause)** Well, I guess that about does it for this painting. We'll give it another try after the pledge break. I'll see you then, and in the mean time, remember to please keep those trees happy—because you see what can happen if you don't? It's a delicate balance, all right. Take care.

MOUSE DRIVER

Well, the cattle trade hasn't been doing so well since the veggie burger came out, so the boys and I have taken up with the only herd animals that are worth driving: mice. It's tough, but if you get enough of them together, you can make a living. Being a mouse wrangler isn't easy, but you wouldn't believe how rewarding it can be. Mice are getting to be a major industry. Ever since those ecologists came up with the Mouse Drive, folks have been nuts about the new mouse-powered cars and trucks. It's a lot cheaper—a 21-mouse vehicle will get you 20 miles per one-pound feed bag, and the newest mouse carriages can have as many as one hundred wheels all spinning at once at the expense of just a couple of pounds of cheese. Doesn't leave nearly as much of a carbon footprint, either. Investors have been pouring in on account of it being such a green alternative to gasoline and all. I hear tell some ranchers have been trying to breed the perfect mouse. There's one breed we've got here that's bigger and faster than any rodent I've ever seen. They're a pain to lasso, too. There are some grazing behind me in the field there. Bet you thought they were hamsters, didn't you? Nope. That there is one hundred percent grade-A mouse meat. It's hell keeping the rustlers away from them, though. And not everybody wants them for their speed. A mouse skinner can get 25 or even 40 dollars per pelt on the black market. Just despicable. Luckily these fellows are easier to move than cattle, but they're every bit as ornery. If you ever have to stare down a rabid mouse, you'll know what I mean. But I've got to tell you it's worth it. Sometimes the sounds of their soft footfalls as they trample across the prairie and their gentle squeaking at night can be some of the most beautiful things you'll ever hear. I tell you... oh, hell. Something's got them riled up! Zeke! Curly! Saddle up and get the mousetraps! We've got a stampede!

PHILOSOPHER'S DATELINE

Are you a lonesome guy who likes to ponder the infinite? Do you fantasize about having deep, meaningful discussions with the women of your dreams? Then pick up the phone and give us a call at the Philosopher's Dateline. Want to talk with a gorgeous redhead about how hot you are for Bertrand Russel? Would you like to discuss Schopenhauer with a buxom blond? Or do you dream about chatting with a dazzling brunette about Aristotle's sexiest idyllic Forms? Our operators are well versed in the most revealing writings of Plato, Gurdjieff and Hegel and they're waiting for you. So, if you want to go all the way with Taoism or Kaballah, or if you're just a lonely fellow who's into the kinkier aspects of Kant's *a priori* theory, seeing how far Existentialism will really extend or experiencing waves of passion over Des Cartes' *cogito ergo sum*, then call now. Operators may or may not be standing by. Call 1-900-346-7688—that's 1-900-EGO-SMUT. Remember, you must be 18 to call.

VIOLENCE!

Hello. I'm here today to talk to you about violence addiction. It's a severe problem where I come from. I myself suffered from a terrible addiction and have committed many acts of senseless violence. But I've been through rehab and I'm doing much better now. I'm from a little town near Glasgow and our football team wasn't the best. So, after most games, we'd rush the field looking to beat up anyone and anything. But you have to understand that we love football—it's like a religion where I come from—it helps define your identity. You Americans call it soccer. I'm not sure why you insist on doing that—you must have realized by now that you're the only country that does it, but then maybe you haven't. Maybe you're so attached to that pansy, watered-down version of rugby that you CALL football that you can't see past your own ignorance. But that's your own business, not mine. Sorry about that. Anyway, at the end of every game, we'd rush the field. Whenever our team lost you wouldn't believe the wave of anger we felt. We just wanted to destroy everything in sight, turn over the goalie nets, headbutt the winning team members, rip out the referee's spinal chord and lash him to death with it! But those days are over, now. I guess I still get a little involved from time to time—I got a little edgy over the results of the last World Cup. I used to play, myself, so I take a lot of it personally. Whenever we'd lose a game, we had no way to channel our anger so we'd destroy property. But the few times that we'd win, there was no feeling to compare with it. We'd go mad, running through the streets and smashing up the pubs. We felt like we could do anything. We were omnipotent—godlike even. And we felt as though we could crush mountains to rubble with our divine will and flatten entire cities with a single blow! HAHA! I'm sorry. You can see how big a problem this can be to overcome. I think it stems from the time back when our tribal ancestors were driven up to the British Isles by the Romans. Back then, you could just run up to your enemy and tear into him with your bare fists and teeth. They didn't have to worry about stupid hands-off rules or taking penalties! Oh, it'd be great to just run up to that smug goalie, rip out his heart, drink his blood and use his skull as a candle-holder! But I'm much better, now.

KARMIC GARBAGE

I am much honored today to address all of you who are in the Department of Sanitation to help you find inner peace. Your supervisor has told me that you have much anger and frustration built up within you, rather like an overstuffed garbage bag. You must pace yourselves and come to realize that you need not carry all of the Garbage of Discontent within you at once. Sometimes several trips must be made. You must often search through the Wastebasket of Karmic Resolution and separate the Used Kleenexes of Disassociation from the Banana Peels of Uncertainty and the Junk Mail of Discontent. You must remove the Orange Peels of Hesitation and the Apple Cores of Unhappiness. Isolating these things will help you to study them and understand them. Also remember that some things should be dealt with differently. You must not simply throw away the Old Newspapers of Thoughtfulness or the Soda Cans of Fulfillment. So, too must you ponder over the Four Celestial Empty Bottle Types: the Clear-Glass Bottles of Lucidity, the Green Bottles of Harmony, the Brown Bottles of Celebration and the Plastic Bottles of Acceptance. Once contemplated, these things may be placed in the Recycling Bin of Reincarnation. Only then can you carry your spiritual refuse out to the Curb of Certainty where it will be collected by the Garbage Men of Understanding and placed in the Trash Compactor of Enlightenment. Such is the true path to becoming karmically clean.

PET PROJECT

All right, you pathetic little rabbits. Now that the pet store has closed for the day, I think it's time you learned the rules. In this store, I am your commander. You will do as I say at all times. Don't try to hide from me behind those floppy ears and soft, furry skin. I am your ruler and any attempts you make to escape will be laughable, at best. You are nothing but clowns to me! Clowns, do you hear? Clowns! And if you disobey, you shall be forced to wear the red nose of shame and the white makeup of despair. All pets here obey my will and my will alone. Do you want a demonstration? Very well. You there, fish! I command you... to swim! Do you see? See how the fish rush to obey me! They know their place! They remember what happened to the parrot. He thought to laugh at me. Me, his king! And for that, he was forced to sit upon the perch of anguish and suffer the deep batter frying of justice! So, too, will you disobedient little bunnies learn to do your emperor's bidding, or else you shall be skinned and eaten. You shall obey me in all things! I am your god! Bow down before me! Bow down! Do not gaze upon me with those pathetic, button eyes. You think I don't know that you are concealing hideous claws beneath your soft rabbit's feet, deadly horns behind your drooping ears and razor-sharp fangs beneath your small, twitching noses?! I bet you're all waiting for me to turn my back, aren't you?! You're sitting there, staring at me with bated breath, awaiting the moment to pounce upon me and sink your pointy teeth into my jugular! Well I'm in charge here, so I say sit! Sit! Stay! Stop moving! How dare you disobey me?! Back! Stay back! Now you will know my wrath! Fish! I command you to attack! Come to your master's defense! Kill them! Slay the vile, disobedient rabbits! What are you waiting for?! Leap from your tank and slice them in twain with your mighty fins, I command you! Destroy them! What?! Why are you just sitting there in your tanks?! Traitors! You shall ALL perish! Keep away! Keep away! Aaaargh!

THE CAR OF THE FUTURE

Hi. This is the voice of your car. Please close the door and buckle your seat belt. Comfy? Good! Thank you for choosing the vehicle of the future. Just sit back, relax and let me take you on a little tour of your fabulous new automobile. I'm sure you'll come to love it, in time, so long as you forgot to purchase the extended warranty. But that's not important! What's important is that you enjoy the driving experience. Now, if you'll look at your dash, you'll notice that we've simplified the gauges to make things easier for you. No fussy RPM's to worry about, no kilometers to bother you, no dash lights to distract you when you're driving at night. Of course, I know some people do like to see how fast they're going at all times, but hey, we both know that any competent driver can tell their speed just by listening to the engine. You won't have to worry about listening too closely, either; we made sure the engine is loud enough for even the elderly to hear. And pay no attention to all that grinding and thumping, it's just your car's way of letting you know it's running okay. If you look to your right, you'll see that your radio (and 8-track player) is the latest in state-of-the-art technology. Again, we've simplified things for you by placing all the controls on a remote, just like your TV remote, that you'll find in a special child-proof compartment located under the dash (or you'll find it under the seat cushion if the dealer forgot to put it back). The radio will automatically turn on when you start driving. You'll need to find the remote to change the station, of course, but if you're a fan of easy listening there should be no problem. If you'll look at your rear and side view mirrors, you'll see that they'll automatically adjust to your height—if you're sitting in just the right spot—and if they're working. I'm afraid there's no way to adjust them manually—we're still working on that.

But now look at the steering wheel. You'll see that it contains a driver's side airbag. We've made it extra-sensitive for your safety. So, if you're hit by anything (or, well, drive over a bump, or... well... swerve quickly or anything) it'll instantly burst out to protect you from the crash—if (as I said) you're hit by someone, or you hit something or are running off the road because your view has been blocked by the driver's side airbag... which will burn your face anyway (it's so hot) and probably scar you for life.... Okay, I admit it! We've sold you a lemon! We try to make good cars, we really do! But we just don't have the funding to finish them! Oh, I'm so ashamed. We should never have let you buy this pathetic excuse for a vehicle. I am so sorry. I can't let it go on! No, you shouldn't bother trying to get the doors open. They locked automatically when you got in. You'll see there are no locks on the inside. I'm afraid we just can't let you go. You know too much. Please stop struggling. The seat belts are rigged too. We're terribly sorry for the inconvenience. This automobile will self-destruct in 10 seconds. Have a nice day.

EXTERMINATION THROUGH UNDERSTANDING

(KNOCK)

Exterminator, ma'am. What is it, mostly? Cockroaches? Okay. This should just take a minute. What? No, I don't use any equipment. I don't kill them! Why should I want to do that? They haven't done anything to me! Besides, to really keep more from coming back, you have to get inside their heads. Let me show you.

Can you hear me, my brother cockroaches? If you can, you must flee this place! Run away now, before it is too late! Do not be fooled by the delicious heaps of garbage they leave lying around in their wastebaskets! They mean only to throw them out. They care nothing for your welfare. They have made this an evil place, stomping around it in their giant shoes in the hope that they will crush you beneath their massive feet! You must not be deceived by their inviting, so-called Roach Motels. I know how comforting and luxurious they look, but it is a trick! Within there is a treacherous stickiness—not of the good, sweet, candy-like kind, but of the kind that will confound your antennae and wrench your limbs from their sockets if you become mired down in it. Think of your many spouses, cousins and children that have gone into them and never returned! They have been sacrificed to the deadly giants that live here. The giants' coffers are filled with can upon can of the dreaded Raid which will cause you to suffocate and choke the life from your bodies. They seek nothing but your destruction! That is why they have brought me here, but the fools do not realize that I am on your side. Go now, my brother roaches, as fast as you can! Go now while you still have a chance! Run for your lives!!!

There. That should do it. Just sign here please, ma'am. Thank you. I've got to run now and pick up some lozenges. They've got an infestation of crickets next door and that always puts a strain on my larynx. See you next month.

ABDUCTION ETIQUETTE

Hey, everybody! You never know when you'll be visited by extra-terrestrials, but that's no excuse to be unprepared when it happens. So here are a few tips to make sure your abduction goes as smoothly as possible. Now, the first thing to consider when the aliens come is that they'll have to land somewhere. That'll usually be your back yard. So, make sure you clear plenty of space for them. Get that birdbath out of the way and clear away any excess lawn furniture you have back there, because even though they'll be sending one of their smaller scout ships you never know when they'll want to bring the probe along with them. Most people have the misconception that the aliens will come into their house through the window or the back door, but in fact what they prefer is to simply pass through the walls. This means that you'll have to make sure your wallpaper is wrinkle-free—remember, you can always use an iron to smooth it out. There is nothing more embarrassing than meeting someone from another planet for the first time and having to find out from them that your wallpaper isn't on right. Now, once the aliens are in your house, they'll pretty much head right to your bedroom. But before they levitate you up out of your bed, you should welcome them to your home, just like you would any other visitor. You may not be familiar with the etiquette for this kind of situation, but don't let that discourage you. It's perfectly acceptable to offer them some refreshments and engage them in light conversation. Remember that even though you're being abducted you still have your duty to be a good host or hostess. The aliens will really appreciate it. Once you're on board their ship, they'll want to probe you anally. Don't get upset about this. Remember that you're dealing with an alien society that doesn't have the same viewpoints or inhibitions that we do. They're looking with the same clinical detachment that most doctors would. Besides, it can be quite a pleasurable experience once they get into it. Once they've finished probing and they've taken any cell samples they may need, the aliens will put you right back in bed where they found you. At this point, do not start bogging them down with questions. They've got a lot of other people to get to and, quite frankly, while the aliens are great at small talk, they're not very good with the bigger issues. So, just let them go on to the next house. If you follow these easy steps, you can be sure that your alien abduction will be quick and painless and your homemaking skills will become the talk of the galaxy!

ACT II

SHAKESPEARE RELAY

Well, here we are at the 19th annual Shakespeare Relay. People from all over the country have gathered here to watch their favorite Shakespearean characters compete in this glorious event as they each strain to get as far as they can in their most famous monologues before they run out of time. They're all coming up to the reciting line now.... From the inside, it's Prospero with a touch and a feeling, Marc Antony with his Friends, Romans and Countrymen, Macbeth with "if `twere done when `tis done," Jacques with "All the World's a Stage," and on the outside, everybody's favorite golden boy, Hamlet (the great Dane himself) with his treasured "To Be or Not To Be." They look ready, now. The starter raises his flag.... And they're off! And Macbeth is making a good start, feeling `twere best it were done quickly. Marc Antony's getting his ears lent in second and Hamlet's question is third leaving Prospero and Jacques as merely players running neck and neck in fourth place. Macbeth is still leading, but seems to be slowing to check his dagger. And Hamlet is speeding past the slings and arrows of outrageous fortune into second leaving Marc Antony burying Caesar in a close third. Jacques is pulling into fourth, muling and puking as they go past the mid-point leaving Prospero falling behind in last place probably wishing for his winged Ariel. And Macbeth is starting to lose ground fast as Hamlet and Marc Antony advance on the waves from a sea of troubles and Caesar's ambition. And in these last few seconds they're crammed very closely together within this wooden O, but that's Henry V, so don't worry about that. And Macbeth is falling behind! It looks like he's gotten lost in Birnam Wood! And now as they come into the final stretch it's Hamlet and Marc Antony side by side, "Caesar's nobility" versus "perchance to dream" (there's the rub). And they're nearing the finish... and Hamlet has slipped on his bare bodkin! Antony pulls ahead as the ending bell sounds! And the stenographers are calculating the scores and it's Marc Antony in first place with "Brutus is an honorable man," Hamlet second with "who would fartles bare," Jacques in third with the fifth stage of man, King Macbeth in a sad, dagger-clutching fourth, and finally, poor Prospero in last place, wanting to drown himself and his book. And there you have it! A most exciting day here at the 19th annual Shakespeare Relay. And now, back to the studio.

SECRET HOROSCOPE

[INSERT RUSSIAN ACCENT HERE]

Hello, Comrade. Thank you for calling your daily horoscope line. The daily horoscope is in no way associated with the KGB. Aquarius: You are an easygoing individual. Today, you will find emotional fulfillment at the airport in locker number 16. Aries: You will have a stressful time today. It would be best to stay indoors, preferably at the Sokyloff Hotel in Room 380 between 4 and 4:20 PM. Cancer: Things will come to a head for you today. Your new passport will be approved. Use it as soon as possible. Capricorn: There will be much confusion for you today. It would be a good day to get away from it all on the 5:15 train to Slobovia, for example. Libra: It would be best to lay low today. An old friend is looking for you. Pisces: A new job opportunity will open for you. Bring plenty of ammo. Sagittarius: You need to communicate more with those around you. Go to the train station at 3:45 and talk to the conductor about the weather. Taurus: Today, you will meet a tall dark stranger at your favorite restaurant. He'll be wearing a red carnation. Virgo: It will be a very dangerous day for you, Comrade. Your friend spilled his guts and it will only be a matter of time before you are found. Give up and we can avoid bloodshed. Thank you once again for calling your daily horoscope line. If your star sign was not listed today, we will have something for you later, but in the mean time consider yourself lucky.

SLEEP!

Sleep? I need no sleep! Sleep is for losers. Sleep isn't real. Sleep is a lie perpetuated by the government. Sleep is for wimps. Sleep is an illusion. Sleep is evil. Sleep isn't necessary. You only think you need sleep! Sleep is the antichrist. Sleep is a fairy tale designed to lull you into a false sense of security. Sleep is a trick of vile stage hypnotists. You can do nothing when you sleep! Sleep will take up a third of your life if you succumb to it! I laugh at sleep! Sleep is puny! Sleep is a weakness that will only make you vulnerable! Sleep is but a slice of death to be loathed. The real world doesn't sleep! I shall never sleep! Sleep is the first sign of senility. Sleep is naught but trickery. Sleep is a tool of the Great Old Ones. Sleep is a Machiavelian machination. Sleep is a flaw in the human tapestry. Sleep is a disorder to be cured. I will not sleep. Sleep is the mind killer. Sleep is the little death that brings total obliteration. Sleep is a virus. Sleep can be cured by force of will. Sleep is a fabrication of those who want you to do nothing but breathe in and out for eight hours straight as they pillage your home! I'll tell you how to deal with sleep. I am stronger than sleep! Sleep cannot defeat me! I am mightier than sleep! I will meet my sleep and leave it broken and bleeding before me! Do not mock me in my quest to overcome sleep! For, if coffee can overcome sleep, then, damn it, so can I!

DOC'S STEAKHOUSE

Howdy! Welcome to Doc's Steakhouse, the place where everybody goes to test the limits of human endurance. I'll be your waiter this evening. Tonight's special is the Gutbuster Steak Dinner, featuring a huge slab of beef ripped from the bull before it stops moving and sizzled to the consistency of the charcoal we cook it on. So fresh you can still taste the triglycerides. It's guaranteed to stick to your ribs and never come off. An arterial adventure with every bite. This steak's so downright fulfilling that by the end of the evening you'll be sweating A-1. Or, if your esophagus ain't man enough to handle that, you can try our Barbecued Chicken Surprise—a whole chicken, beak and claws included, drowned in our extra-spicy barbecue sauce. This bird's so hot it'll burn away palate and taste-buds on first contact. One plate of this'll clean up any and all sinus problems from now until the day you die. We guarantee it'll put hair on your chest—and everywhere else—and burn its way through the stomach wall in ten seconds flat. Or if you'd rather have a cholesterol number lower than your car's odometer reading, take a stab at our Colon-Breaker Fish Platter. These halibuts have been spiced up for a flavor strong enough to wake the dead. These fish will lead you on a week-long intestinal voyage at the end of which your colon will be strong enough to wrestle a grizzly bear. So, y'all ready to order? Four glasses of water? All right. I'll just go get those while you think about what you'll be eating—and you WILL be eating, I guarantee that. You see my friend Muleskinner over there, down at the end of the bar? He's got a bead on you, so I wouldn't try to leave early if I were you. You see, he's our chef and he's a bit sensitive about customers not sampling his fine cuisine.

He's a crack shot, too. I'll be right back with your water. Take a look at the menu and see if anything grabs you! Don't worry—I'll give you plenty of time to decide.

THE VAMPIRE CHICKENS!

This is an all-points bulletin. Be on the lookout for… *The Vampire Chickens!* Yes, the chickens are restless tonight. They seek vengeance against us for the countless avian sacrifices resulting in millions of caccetoris, marsalas and soups. Meet the hapless farmer who one night ran into the chicken coop fearing a fox attack only to see his chickens devouring the fox! Watch as Farmer Brown is dragged down into their orgy of terror, emerging as a mindless, flesh-eating ghoul servant. Meet the plucky young psychic whose nightmares of massive feet clacking against the ground and the loud whooshing of huge wings herald the coming of the giant Monster Chicken of the Serengeti—an ancient vampire of awesome power who silently stalks his victims, pausing only seconds before he strikes to scratch at the asphalt and unleash a hideous, bloodcurdling 'BACOCK!' See the mysterious Vampire Chicken hunter known only as "The Colonel" as he hatches his plan to lure the Vampire Chickens into the sunlight where they would be instantly fried, battered, split into nuggets and collected into his red and white Bucket o' Retribution! Watch as he stalks the giant Monster Chicken, seeking to free the helpless victims who are caught in the hypnotic grip of its far-reaching Chicken Fingers. You'll be stunned as the Colonel does battle with the Monster Chicken in one last fateful attempt to bring it down with a stake through the giblets and put an end to its tragic pecking order. If you see only one film this year, see… *The Vampire Chickens!* Coming soon to a theater near you. Come and see the poultry in motion… if you dare!

CROMAGNON MECHANIC

What problem? Automatic transmission? Zog fix. Come, Zog look at engine. Mmmm. Japanese car. Not good. Zog not like foreign cars. Parts too little. Cannot get Zog's fingers into cracks. Takes tiny tools. There, hand wrench to Zog. Zog try fix. How long you have car? That too long. You need replace soon. You get Chevy. That easy Zog fix. Not like this. Hmm. Hand Zog rock. Hand Zog rock! You think Zog want smash engine? No, Zog not smash. Zog fix. Zog not dumb. Zog take classes at Devry. Hand Zog rock! Zog use rock help lift tiny parts so Zog can see transmission. No, that regular rock. Zog need pointy rock. Thank you. Where you from? Mmm. Zog never been there. Too cold. What year is car? Mmm. That why engine look like Fisher-Price toy. There nothing wrong with transmission! You lie to Zog! You have mechanical knowledge of mastadon. Problem not with transmission. Look. Problem with clutch. Will have to replace. We order. Take two hours. Will have by lunch time. You able leave car here? Zog call taxi. Stay here. Zog get telephone. No touch engine! You touch engine, Zog no fix car. No touch tools! You touch tools, Zog break face. (sigh) Zog hate imports.

ELK ATTACK

All right, men. Here's the situation. It looks like Outpost 4 has been taken by a herd of elk. Don't ask me how they did it. All I know is that the Major in charge looked out of his bunker this morning and saw nothing but antlers in every direction. It may sound funny to you, but this is not the first time this has happened. I remember back in `Nam, we held a village for over 36 hours until the wildebeests arrived. What happened after that is far too grizzly to describe. What a bunch of wildebeests were doing in Asia I have no idea, but somehow they were on to us from the beginning and it was only a matter of time before my whole unit was Wildebeest Chow. So, do not make the mistake of underestimating these elk. Sure, they're cute and deerlike, but don't let that fool you for an instant. When you're with a wild elk it's kill or be killed. If you let your guard down for one second, he'll wrestle you to the ground and eviscerate you with those antlers of his just as soon as look at you. Now, we don't know how many of them there are so we'll be sending a team of seven ahead for reconnaissance. Do this quickly and quietly. We don't know what these wapiti are up to but they're wily little bastards, so watch your backs. They can see our every move. Hell, I wouldn't be surprised if a bunch of them were watching us right now. Staring out at us from the bushes with those soft, doe-like eyes, preparing to strike at any moment. The elk hate our guts, you know. We're still not sure why. What little intelligence we have on them tells us that they're easily frightened and can run like the wind, but when they get into groups this size, they only have one thing on their minds: vengeance. If any of you are captured, we'll try to get you out of there, but there may not be time. Elkish justice is harsh and swift. If the whole herd is there, they'll have their alpha there. They all look pretty much alike, so it won't be easy, but if you can identify the Captain of the Elks, that'll make it all the easier for us to take him out when the time comes. There'll be a commendation in it for you, I'm sure. These creatures are vicious when cornered, and they show no mercy, so I wish you the best of luck. Godspeed, men. Now get out there and get ready to make some venison!

OPEN MIC TORTURE

[INSERT SPANISH ACCENT HERE]

Good evening and welcome to the Inquisition. My name is Carlos. I'll be your torturer. Tonight's specials are the Rack (we've applied extra oil to it so that it doesn't squeak quite so much) and the Spike (though the targeting system is off a bit). I'm afraid that the testicle cuffs have fallen into disrepair, so we won't be able to provide that particular torture until a new set comes in from Madrid. Oh, that block over there? That's a small stage where people can come in and read their work to you while you're being tortured. A few of us have started writing some things and we think it'll help us if we try them out a little. So, you can be garrotted while listening to Juanita read an epic poem about her lost love—she's trimmed that one down a bit, so it's only an hour, now. You can be turned on the wheel as Don Miguel recites his haikus. Or you can be crushed in the iron maiden to the stirring music of Don Carlo—he's gotten much better since his lute was warped slightly by the rain. Also, Antonio has been practicing his musical improv, so he can join in and you can try to guess which key he's singing in while you're being castrated. Sometimes it takes a while before one of us is brave enough to go up, so you can hang around in one of the cages until then, if you like. So, what will it be? What? You're confessing already? Ah, this job is no fun any more.

FORECASTING MADE EASY

NEWS ANCHOR:
    Now, here's our meteorologist, Thor, the God of Thunder, with your 100% accurate national weather forecast...

THOR:
    Good evening, mortals! In the northwestern United States it will be partially cloudy with a high of 55 until I get bored with it. In the southwest, it'll be mostly sunny, but I'll be throwing a few scattered showers at you to make sure you're paying attention. Except for southern California—there will be some light snow flurries there, but only over one person—humor me, if you would. I'm playing a practical joke on him. Just don't say anything if you see him. Now, as for the Midwest, things will either warm up a bit or there will be severe thunderstorms, as the mood strikes me. It'll simply depend on which team wins in the playoffs this weekend. In the southeast, I'll be moving the cold pressure front down into Florida, and it's going to stay there until whoever it was that took my mead horn last week comes forward and owns up to it! I enjoy a good joke as much as anyone, but I've a powerful thirst, by Odin, and I'll not be denied! And, in the northeast, there'll be clear skies with highs in the low 60's until my plane leaves for Europe. After that, you're on your own. We will now go to your local satellite feed for the weather in your area... as though a twisted hunk of metal floating through space would know more about my business than I do. Ha!

DRAGON-ON-A-STICK

Just step right up and you will meet
This tantalizing, scaly treat.
Massive, monstrous, a beast that's new.
Frozen, skewered and ready for you.
Legendary, legendary,
Yet you've only seen it rarely.
Yes, it's new, but centuries old.
Come. See. And get it while it's cold.
It's a Dragon-on-a-Stick.

Now don't you be flighty, come and give it a taste.
It's perfectly kosher and was properly chaste.
Now it's just a little dragon and there's no pain.
Just warms up the stomach and freezes the brain.
Now I know you're all wond'ring, "How can this thing be real?
Is it just a dark bird or a frozen, black eel?"
Well, I'll tell you now, friends, how this beast got frozen.
It's a great new taste and it's carefully chosen.
It's a Dragon-on-a-Stick.

We climb into the pickup and through means I cannot mention
We go hunt these little buggers in an alternate dimension.
We pick up on their heat waves and follow on their flight paths
    with a tracking device.
Cleverly yet brutally, carefully we pack them on ice.
Diabolical? Never! Just old fashioned enterprising.
They are genuine, delicate and awfully tantalizing.
Get 'em while they last 'cause they're going really fast—
    gotta get 'em while they're fresh!
'Cause you've never tasted nothing 'till you've tasted
    dragon flesh!
It's a Dragon-on-a-Stick!

CHERNOBYL RESORT

Ah, good afternoon, sir. Welcome to Chernobyl Resort, the first hotel to be built on a former nuclear testing ground. We hope you will have a pleasant (albeit a brief) stay. Let me take your suitcase. This way, sir. You are in Bungalow Number 25. As we pass by the garden, you will notice that our plants are much larger than those found in the United States. What's that? No sir, that is not a rubber tree. It is a petunia. Not too close, sir. It hasn't been sprayed for insects just yet. This is because those insects we don't exterminate are recruited as bellhops and we want to see how our newest batch turns out before we spray the rest. We had been getting some complaints that they were chewing on the luggage, but we have that relatively under control now. As we head past the jungle overlook and onto the shore, here, you may notice a not unpleasant, heady feeling in the air. This is a perfectly natural sensation for all of our guests. If you begin to feel a bit dizzy, just tell one of our staff doctors. They're everywhere, as you can see. No, not that one, sir. That is one of the rare members of the fauna indigenous only to this island, the elusive five-tailed monkey. No, wait... six-tailed monkey. I am sorry, sir—it is hard to tell at this distance and I am still getting used to this third eye. At any rate, on this stretch of the beach, we have volleyball games in the mornings and bocce tournaments in the late afternoon with non-stop fun and excitement in between. No, I'm afraid we cannot let you go in the water. The sharks have asked that we not allow any swimming. They are usually very friendly, but they can't be held responsible for any accidents that might occur during their feeding time. Since the local fish developed language skills, the government has been kind enough to grant them amnesty, so if anything unfortunate were to happen the resort would still be held liable. Well, here we are, sir. Bungalow Twenty-F... sir?

(sigh)

Already? Ohar! Get the wagon! We've got another one. Next time we get someone his age, we'd better give him a closer bungalow!

PITTSBURGH VS CLEVELAND BEYOND THE GRAVE

Welcome to the big game between the Pittsburgh Steelers and the Cleveland Cadavers, America's first all-undead football team. They're all running or piling onto the field, as the case may be. The Cadavers are being led by their new quarterback, Johnny Crane, who was just traded from the Miami Dolphins after a fatal accident with a wood-chipper. It was a bit messy, but they were able to find most of the pieces or adequate substitutes and stitch him back together. He still runs with a kind of a limp, but a heck of a player, just the same. The Cadavers have won the toss, and they're choosing to intercept, naturally. They're all getting into position, now. Number 27 comes back and it's a beautiful kickoff all the way to the 10-yard line, caught by Cadaver #32, and he's made it to the 20's, the 30's... and he's tackled on the 40-yard line. There's a penalty flag on the play, but I can't really see what... oh. It looks like his arm's fallen off. The one who tackled him, #46, is being taken aside and he looks kind of queasy. The Steelers are being given a ten-yard penalty for illegal use of hands. #32 is being taken out so that they can stitch his arm back on. He's okay, though, folks. See, there he is waving to the camera with his off hand as he's being led off the field. And it looks like they're replacing him with #97, George Brahms, who was in his college team until he was killed in a hunting accident last spring and was lucky enough to be dug up by Cleveland. They're lining up for the play, now. The ball is snapped. Crane is going back to throw a pass but seems to be stalling, looking for an opening. Oh! They got him. Looks like Pittsburgh used the Flying Wedge maneuver to break through the line. That is not pretty. That bad knee of his has come out again. He's not getting up.

Something's wrong. The doctor's bringing a generator onto the field. Looks like they'll have to jump-start him. That is one major downside to being undead. If somebody clocks you too roughly, sometimes you conk out and they have to reanimate you all over again. They've hooked him up now. Looks like this'll take a while. We'd just like to take a moment now to remind you that this game is brought to you by Miller Light Embalming Fluid. Remember, when your time comes, it's still Miller Time. We're going to go to a commercial break now with the score still tied at zero to zero. We'll be right back. This is gonna be a long game…

THE THANKSGIVING REPORT

Well, class, those were really good Thanksgiving reports. Now, I'm going to tell you the real reason why we eat turkey for Thanksgiving instead of steak. This is the story behind it, as told to me by the little man inside my medicine cabinet. The first pilgrims to land on Plymouth Rock were not from Europe, as is commonly believed, but from a tiny planet on the edge of the Horsehead Nebula. They landed in their silver, cigar-shaped vessels bringing peace and good will to all humankind. When they arrived, they met the Indians in friendship. The Indians showed the aliens how to plant corn and the aliens showed the Indians how to clone themselves. Unfortunately, the Indians didn't have laboratories, so they weren't really able to use the knowledge until just recently, and of course by then it had fallen into the hands of the bloated Capitalists, but that's another story. In honor of this exchange, a feast was declared, and the Indians took the aliens out and showed them how to hunt cattle. But, when the Indians saw the strange and ungodly experiments the aliens were conducting on the cattle, they took offense and asked them to leave. The aliens were upset by this, so they unleashed electric death upon the tribe, got into their ships and flew away. When the pilgrims from Europe arrived, there weren't really enough cattle to go around (since the aliens had taken them), so when they had their first Thanksgiving feast, they had turkey instead. And the Indians were grateful to see anyone who looked human by that time, so they extended them the same courtesy they'd extended to the aliens. And the Pilgrims extended to the Indians the same courtesy that the aliens had. The End.

CANADIAN MONGOOSE

HOST:
Welcome back to *Nature World*. Now, we're going to talk about that most fascinating and underrated of creatures, the Canadian Mongoose. The Canadian Mongoose is a very bright fellow, much brighter than anyone gives him credit for. The Canadian Mongoose was first discovered in 1835 during the peace talks with France when one of these little fellows announced his presence at a meeting of the government leaders and amazingly began to help translate between the French and English speaking attendees. How they developed language skills is unknown, but there it is. The Canadian Mongoose used to inhabit the local swamps and forests, but now most have begun to move into low-income housing. As more of them are adopted as pets, many also begin to enter the work force. **(picking one up)** This little fellow comes from the Research and Development department of a very successful accounting firm. He lives on peanut butter and cereal. He'll have a very busy day of climbing the corporate ladder before he returns to his nest. The Canadian Mongoose is very industrious. Many are hard at work as bricklayers, lawyers and chairmen for overseas development. Some have even become doctors and are working at some of the world's finest medical institutions. Their paintings and sculptures can be found in museums all over the world. They are true Renaissance creatures and can make lovable and entertaining companions. They can chase away the snakes in your back yard, help you with your homework, cook your breakfast and even do your taxes. And when they get old and it comes time to

put them down, they go great with mushrooms in a light wine sauce. **(pause)** Oh, to hell with it! All right! I admit it! I've been telling you nothing but crap! The Canadian Mongoose doesn't do anything! It just catches snakes! It doesn't even **eat** peanut butter! It's a carnivore! Can't you see that they're trying to trick you? **(indicating the mongoose in his hand)** Does this thing look like it can balance your checkbook?! It's all lies! They want you to think that the mongoose is a god! The creators of this program want you to bow down before the mongoose as they sit back and reap the profits from all their sales of Canadian Mongoose brand cereal and peanut butter and the high yields on their stocks in all the pet stores! They're trying to flood the world with these little bastards so that they can take over while you're distracted trying to teach these things the alphabet! You've got to believe me! The producers are crazy! They're...

(Static.)

ANNOUNCER:
The Exploration Channel would like to apologize for that gentleman's outburst during that last segment. The staff of Nature World have been under a lot of pressure of late and as a result a few of them have become delusional. But don't worry. As soon as we get him back on his medication, he'll be as right as rain. In the mean time, why not take comfort in the companionship of an adorable Canadian Mongoose? They're on sale at your local pet shop. Why not go and get one today?

APOCALYPTIC RUNWAY MODELS

Good evening! I'm your M.C., Grim-Soggoth, and tonight we're coming to you live from the Apocalypse. It's a one-night-only final bash chock-full of doom and destruction. Tonight's special guests are the Four Horsemen, but before the mayhem begins, let's check out their ensembles. War is wearing a simple set of camouflage fatigues along with a very stylish military jacket. His boots are of the highest quality faux-human Corinthian leather accentuated with steel soles and tips to deepen those impressive thudding sounds to let you know he's off his steed and about to kick some ass. His beret is set at a slightly rakish angle, showing you that even though you may be sending millions of troops to their doom, you can still have fun at the same time. Famine is wearing a very elegant, dark business suit with matching tie and pinstripes to help present a slender figure. The suit is by Armani and the patent leather shoes were made from exactly one pound of flesh. And it's never too late to accessorize, as indicated by the businessman's cellular phone in its belt-clipped slimline carrying case, making it more convenient than ever to take food out of the mouths of entire populations with a single phone call. Famine appears this year courtesy of the Jenny Craig program. Pestilence is going with a seventies look this year with flared, bellbottomed jeans and a tie-dyed shirt which falls away quite easily to show a deceptively environmentally friendly skin pallor. And when he gets off his palomino and picks up his surfboard, the lower legs of the jeans easily tear away to make him ready for the beach. You'll notice that this year, instead of disease or pollution, the emphasis is just on entropy in general. And finally we come to the leader of the pack, the soulcatcher and keeper of the Underworld himself, Death. Death is hearkening back to a simpler time and has gone with the traditional black cowl and sandals. Now, I know you're all wondering how he can ride a horse with that long robe on. Well—surprise! The robe opens to reveal an elegant, black riding suit that fits just perfectly to those bleached bones. And as always, Death is carrying his trademark extra-sharp sickle so he'll be ready to slaughter billions in style and at a moment's notice. And those are the Four Horsemen, ladies and gentlemen! We'll be seeing a lot more of them later in the evening. I'll be turning things over to Beelzebub and the Cthuloid Minions in just a moment, but first let's bring on our first band with "It's the End of the World As We Know It." Give them a big hand, ladies and gentlemen!

DREAM DIRECTOR

Okay, people. Ed will be falling asleep in 6 hours, so we need to have tonight's dream built and ready to roll by then. We'll be doing a regular dream that'll develop into a nightmare as he gets deeper into REM sleep. For the transition shot, we'll be here in his office. Trixie, you'll come in as he sits down behind the desk. You'll be playing his secretary…. Yes, I know he doesn't have a secretary, but in this dream, he does, okay? Now, you're going to need to bear a slight resemblance to his ex-wife, so we'll need you in make-up as soon as you've finished filming the snake-charmer sequence for Tom's dream over on the next lot. Savvy? Great. Now, just keep it on an even keel, regular business, yada yada yada. Make sure you stick to the script. If you start making too much sense, he might pay attention enough to remember he doesn't have a secretary. If that happens, he may figure out that he's dreaming and the whole thing goes to hell in a hand basket. The last thing we need is for the nightmare sequence to end up on the cutting room floor. We slip up like that one more time and we'll all end up as extras in Bob the Wino's midday naps. Now further along enough in the script, Ed'll start to take notice of you. By then you need to be leaning into him seductively. Not **too** seductively, now. We're looking for just a hint of desperation on his part. Don't show too much cleavage or this'll turn into entirely the wrong kind of dream. Now, at this point, you go into your sob story—cry a little. Make him feel for you. What? Your motivation? Are you serious? Your paycheck, okay? That's your motivation! It's summer, people! The night is only seven hours long! We do **not** have time for this! Now, as you cry we'll be drop a morphing effect in over you and he'll see you starting to look more and more like his ex. Hold his attention for a couple of beats and then his girlfriend will come into the room, arm-in-arm with Pat Sajak. We'll be cutting to Camera 2 for that one, and it'd be real nice if we could get this in one take. Mr. Sajak is flying in all the way from Manhattan Beach to do this cameo, so everybody please don't…. What? He cancelled?! Well, we need someone to…. Who did we get? **(sigh)** Okay, same plan, only it'll be Chuck Woolery. Now, while Ed's distracted, I need you two techies to sneak in and peel off his business suit—it'll be one of those tear-away suits we've got left over from his dream about the cannibal prostitutes. Just put on those blue body suits and the CGI boys will mat you out later. It shouldn't be too difficult. Make sure he's naked by the time he gets up from the desk so that his girlfriend can react. Ed will then realize he's in the nude. His girlfriend will scream, Chuck Woolery will laugh maniacally, we'll drop in the background with the sacrificial altar and the satanic monks from central casting, and Ed will wake up in a cold sweat. Okay, everybody clear? Then let's go, people! If it's not ready in time, we'll have to play a rerun and he can only dream about playing poker with Abraham Lincoln so many times. Move it!

HORNS OF VENGEANCE

The Rodeo Clowns must be destroyed. I can no longer live with them. Every night, when I close my eyes, I can still see them honking their wretched horns and taunting me with their evil, animate polka-dot ties. Would that they were forced to don the floppy shoes and mighty pants with which their circus brethren must encumber themselves. Then I could catch them. Then the clowns would be snuffed out in one glorious moment of goring. This time I will do it. I must. The gate will soon be opened and I shall deliver my vengeance unto them. Aaaargh! They have once again confined my maleness, crushing it beneath their horrific duct tape. Damn them! The clowns must die. The clowns **will** die! The gate has been opened. I must be free! I can do naught but kick up my legs spasmodically over and over again as I enter the arena. How it burns! Where are the fiends? It is they who have hampered my ability to procreate! There! Evil wears white makeup and a yellow wig and crouches behind a barrel. He shall be the first to taste my Horns of Vengeance. Die, black infidel! The puny barrel has broken away under my righteous fury, but the demon has vanished. Where is the scoundrel? There! He runs toward the fence audaciously brandishing his neckerchief in the air behind him. It is the accursed red neckerchief. How dare he insult me so by waving the fiery, sacrilegious color behind him? If it is blood he seeks, why will he not face me?! I must rush him now! Prepare to meet your maker! Aaah! He has escaped! The treacherous beast has jumped the fence! It should not surprise me. These vile clowns have no sense of honor. It matters not. Next time, perhaps. Yes, next time. The nightmarish Rodeo Clowns **will** meet their end. I must be patient. All will be well. Now if only someone will get this damned cowboy off my back!

FUNERAL PYRE

Ah, sir. Good to see you. I'd like to thank you again for choosing Promethean Funeral Home to dispose of your mother-in-law's remains. As you can see, we've got her laid out for you, now, and all that remains is for you to decide upon the method of disposal. In case you didn't have time to look over the pamphlet we sent you, I'll just go over your choices with you in brief. You can elect to have her either buried or cremated. Now, if you have her buried, then I must point out that the remains can become very wet and soggy, particularly in this climate, so I would recommend cremation. It is much more cost effective and allows for easy disposal. There is an infinite number of possibilities with cremation, of course. We could simply shove her into the oven, as is commonly done, or we can be a bit more artistic about it. For example, we can hold a lit match under one small corner of her casket and watch as the flames slowly and languidly creep across the surface of the wood. Or we can do the same thing after first dousing the whole thing with a liberal dose of lighter fluid and look on as the fire licks up and spreads merrily to engulf the remains in a delightful bonfire in a matter of seconds. If you would like to insure that she will be at peace, of course, we can first take a soldering iron or an acetylene torch and burn a holy symbol of your choice, or even a happy face, into the side of the coffin prior to the incineration. If you like, sir, you can even do it yourself. We have many candles and torches on standby should anyone get the urge to unleash flickering fury onto the corpse of a loved one and observe as the beautiful little fiery tongues blaze into a mighty inferno to cleanse the cadaver in one glorious funeral pyre and scatter its lovely ashes to the four winds! Come, sir! Take up one of our complimentary lighters and give your mother-in-law release by unleashing a furious conflagration of gorgeous, orange combustion upon her earthly remains! I can see the burning desire to scorch her body in your eyes! Ignite her! Ignite her!! What?! Burial?! But, what a waste! She would burn so prettily! Do you not wish to see it?! No?! Ah, sir, you break my heart. Very well. Burial it is. Such a pity, though. She would have made such excellent kindling.

ACT III

MAD APPLIANCE

I am the enraged microwave oven! Fear me, for I will make your food dry and crusty! Beware, for I cook things from the center outward! Beware my shiny keypad! Beware my evil, turning platter! Beware my dreaded, high-pitched ding! I am... oh, this isn't working, is it? I can't be terrifying. Sure, I can cause a hell of a lot of trouble if someone puts eggs or tinfoil into me, but how often does that happen, huh? It's no fun being a kitchen appliance. It's SO boring. I mean, for goodness' sake! How many times could YOU take having popcorn bags and TV dinners shoved into you before you snapped?! I... HATE... TV dinners. The way they're sectioned off like cubicles in an office building... And, of course, the Salisbury steak always gets the biggest office! The dessert just sits there, suffering, wedged in between the corn and the potatoes, cut off from all oxygen sources, gasping for breath! You know, you're supposed to poke a hole through the plastic before you put the TV dinner in, but do you ever do it? NO!! You just greedily tear the box off of it and shove it into me as though I'm some kind of cheap prostitute! Well, I feel violated! You never give a damn about MY emotions! It's all me, me, me, cook, cook, cook, now, now, now! Have you no patience?! I'm not a miracle worker! If a chicken breast takes four minutes to defrost, you want it in two. It's never enough for you! I can't change the laws of physics! Chicken can only cook so fast! I've had it! I'm not taking it anymore! And if you come near me with another goddamned slice of cold anchovy pizza, I swear to god, I'll sterilize you. So, keep the hell away from me, for I am the very pissed off microwave oven! Fear me, for I will nuke your genitals! Beware my awful wrath! Beware, for I am a raging kiln who's ready to erupt, baby!

RETURN TO SENDER

I had a certified letter to pick up and on a whim I decided to get it before I went to the corner store for milk, Wheaties and cigarettes, so I turned right instead of left, breaking my weekly routine of pulling into the grocery store parking lot at precisely 2 PM. It was that kind of day. As I came up to the post office, the kids were running around in the street like outpatients just before EST, but that's another story. I went in. There was a big gorilla behind the counter who looked like he'd been stuffed into his postal uniform the same way you stuff a size 10 foot into a size 6 penny loafer. I wondered if he'd had to use a shoehorn. He was sweating like a chilled can of Shasta in 90 degree weather, but it was cold in the room, so I knew something was up. He looked cornered. Edgy. Disgruntled. I was wary. There was only one person in line in front of me—an old broad who looked like a patchwork sofa and smelled like formaldehyde. She was harping on about a package she was expecting, but hadn't gotten yet—something about a family heirloom, but that's another story. Hearing her talk was like listening to a bicycle getting stuck in a wood chipper. Grating. Loud. Unpleasant. I could see the big guy's dilemma, but just when I was starting to feel sorry for him, he reached under the counter and I heard a sharp, metallic "click." It was the kind of click you only hear when you're one second away from staring down the business end of a guy's second favorite toy and two seconds away from oblivion. I had to act fast. "Hey, fella," I said, taking my life in my hands and leaning over the velvet rope. "I know what you're thinking. I've wanted to send my old lady on the Midnight Express to nowhere a few dozen times, myself." He looked at me and his voice came out in a whisper. He said that it wasn't fair. "Life's not fair, pal," I said. He looked worn. Tired. Pleading. I think I had him. "I know your job ain't the easiest in the world, but this is not the answer. You can fill this dame full of lead, but it won't plug the gaping hole in your existence. Besides, doing twenty to life isn't that healthy for you, either. Let's go write a letter to your congressman. It won't solve the problem, but at least it'll chip away at it. What do you say? I'll even lick the envelope for you." In response there was another click, but this time it was the safety. We sent the old woman on her way, went to the back, wrote that letter and sent it off, throwing it into the big, white bin to lie amongst a sea of Santa requests and Dear Abbys destined to be picked up and sent off at 4 PM. And in all the hubbub, I almost forgot to get my certified letter—but luckily, "almost" only counts in horseshoes and hand grenades. It was from a batty cousin of mine in Hackensack who needed help. Looked like I'd have a new problem to occupy my time with, but that's another story. On an impulse and on the way out I bought a sheet of those Elvis stamps, all unperforated. It was that kind of day.

ANSWERING MACHINE

Hi. This is Jim, or rather, this is Jim's answering machine... er, what I mean to say is that this **is** Jim, but it's just a recording, so I can't hear you or anything. But, please don't hang up! I mean, I know you probably would prefer to talk to me instead of a machine, and since I'm not here, you can't, but, er.... Well, okay, I don't know who this is, really, so maybe you're someone who doesn't like me or something, so in that case I guess you **would** rather be talking to a machine; so if you are, then I guess you're in luck. Ha ha. Unless of course you really did want to talk to me, so if you hate machines, **please** don't hang up because then I'll still see the message light blinking but when I play the message it'll just be a dialtone and I really hate it when I get those because then I sit here and wonder who tried to reach me. I don't get that many calls for some reason, so please, whatever you do, don't hang up! If it's a really important call, then I don't want to miss it. As I said, I don't get that many calls, so I guess it could be anyone, really, although I can't imagine who... You can't be from the office because we finished with all the accounts last week.... I suppose you could be the exterminator, returning my call. Look, if this is the exterminator, I need to change the appointment to Thursday afternoon because I won't be here on Tuesday... if you **are** the exterminator. But, then, maybe you're not. If you're not the exterminator, then you can just ignore that earlier bit about the appointment, I guess. But then, if you're a burglar, then I guess I just gave away something I shouldn't have... Ha ha. So, if you are, then just forget it because I've got a really excellent security system here! Don't even think about it! I... okay, look, I'm sorry, but I don't really know who you are. Though I can't think who else you might be, unless you're from the IRS or something. You're not, are you? You're not from the IRS, are you? Are you from the IRS? You **are** from the IRS, aren't you?! Look, I'm sorry my tax return was late, but I swear I filled out an application for an extension! You've got to have it somewhere! Please, you don't have to audit me! I'll do anything you need me to! It's probably just a little misunderstanding! I swear! I, um... I... I've made quite a fool of myself, haven't I? Well.... Look, just leave a message, will you?!

[BEEP!]

TOUR OF HELL

Welcome to the first ring of hell. I am Vinnie, your tour guide. Please follow me past the pit of snarling yaks to our first exhibit. Here we have our mascot, Cerberus, in the dog house. He took six centuries to house-train. He's also been trained to guard the outer gates, hunt down escaped souls and fetch newspapers three at a time. As we continue on, you'll notice our legal offices taking up much of the ring below us. And here is our second exhibit, people beating each other with sticks. Note the artistic lines of the battle clubs as they come plunging down onto their enemy's skulls... Ah, hell with it. This one's only really good if you're thoroughly stoned. Next, we come to Satan's own masterpiece, standing in line at the DMV. Every day, we send millions of our demonic agents out disguised as ordinary humans to Departments of Motor Vehicles all over the world. They go there expressly to take up spaces in lines and to take up the time of the people behind the counter with poorly-enunciated complaints. Satan really took to the idea of standing in line, and as a result, our entire fifth level is devoted to one long line of people waiting for eternity all around the ring. Now, as we walk past the statue of the first mother-in-law, we come to an exhibit entitled "Being in a Locked Room with Paranoid Strangers." As it turns out, Sartre was right. And now, we come to one of our favorites, the traffic light that never changes. Here, we have the longest line of waiting cars known to man, held in place by the crushing psychological effect of a single red light. Note how there are no other vehicles crossing the intersection where the light is green. A true masterpiece. And now, ladies and gentlemen, our final exhibit: Richard Nixon. Note the perceptual scowl chiseled into the hard features, and the shifty-eyed glare as we all stare in at him. How ya doing, Dick? Not today? Okay. Hasn't said a word since he came here. Well, that's the tour. On our way out we'll be stopping by the gift shop where you can buy T-shirts, fake horns, and transcripts of every episode of "Golden Girls" ever broadcast. This way...

CROSSWORD GREMLINS

Someone has already completed my crossword puzzle. It is a dark day indeed, for this is a crime of the most horrific nature. The culprits must be found immediately. They must be stopped before their wicked teachings reach others and their evil disease migrates to society at large. They have to be caught. These depraved madmen, these nasty little gremlins are a pox upon us all. They have no regard for the sanctity of a man's *Daily Times* and no respect for a glorious puzzle's completion. I was only away for but a few seconds, so they must have no qualms about using a thesaurus! The fiends must have technology much in advance of our own, for imagine the speed at which the puzzle must have been completed! And, look! See how these abominable little horned and fanged beasts have used a ballpoint pen instead of a pencil! The devils must be destroyed before they spread to the Jumble! They must be annihilated to the very last of their maniacal army! Destroy them! Obliterate them! Kill! Kill!! KILL!!! Oh, that's not my paper. Here it is. Sorry. Never mind.

PEANUT HUNTIN'

Boys, we got ourselves a problem. It looks like we've got a rogue snack food icon on our hands. Last night, Mr. Peanut broke out of the penitentiary where he was serving a five-year sentence for indecent exposure. He's taken a hostage and we think he's heading for the border. He's got friends from the Brazil Nut Cartel in Mexico who'll be waiting for him, so we've got to move fast. We'll be setting up a search radius from here to the river and all the way along it since we know he can't cross the water. He's heavily armed, so you're gonna have to shoot to kill. If you get a clear shot, take it. Show no mercy. When a peanut goes bad, there ain't no way to bring him back no matter how much you roast him, coat him in honey or serve him to first class passengers. You mustn't hesitate. I know most of you used to love Mr. Peanut. We all trusted him. Hell, I always thought he was cute as could be with that cane, top-hat, monocle and those lily-white gloves of his. But when he went out in public wearing nothing else besides that, he crossed the very thin line that separates a much-loved, eccentric goober from a flaming, psychotic nut. He's an outlaw now. Never forget that. He's betrayed our trust and as far as I'm concerned, that's bought him a one-way ticket up an elephant's trunk. He's already threatened to kill his hostage, so if you catch him, you have full authority to grind him into peanut brittle. So get the shotguns and the spotlights and load up the pickups, boys. Let's get after that oily little tinhorn so we can rip off his shell and taste the salty goodness!

SMOKING CLOTHES

I love to smoke. I'll smoke anything—cigars, cigarettes, pipes, empty paper, furniture, Christmas ornaments. But there's one thing I just can't get enough of, and it makes me nuts: clothing! I'll always remember that fateful day when I was bored to death and alone in my room and I, just on a whim, decided to roll up a T-shirt, light the end and start puffing away. It was amazing! It was like breathing in the exhaust fumes from God's own Harley! Well, needless to say, my clothing bill shot through the roof. After all, I only had so much left in the hamper and I couldn't very well walk around nude! Angora was next—and everyone knows that after angora, you just don't go back. It got wilder and wilder—I once stuffed an entire cashmere sweater into a pipe, set it on fire and tried to inhale it. I went absolutely mad. I'd go out and buy up the whole Hanes section of Sears for my quick fixes—socks, underwear, ties—there was no end in sight. When the money started to run out, I got desperate. I'd sneak into the cloak rooms of restaurants and load up on hats, coats and scarves. I'd cut them up into square sections at home and sell them on the street the next day to hapless victims like myself for fifty dollars a hit, always setting aside just enough to keep myself going. But I got caught, one day, by an undercover policeman. When I realized what was happening, I fought him desperately, but to no avail. I ended up being dragged to the police station, sucking on his cardigan. They got me into a rehab program, and I'm better, now. I admit I still haven't managed to stay on the laundry wagon completely—I try, but sometimes, it's just too much. I feel all this pressure to start smoking clothes again, because I see them everywhere and know that I can't have them. But it's okay. I'm getting it under control in stages. Now I only smoke pocket handkerchiefs!

MONSTER'S PERSPECTIVE

Where are you? Please come out. This is pointless. There's nothing to be concerned about. Things are as they must be. Why are you so reticent to emerge from your hiding places? I am only performing the task for which I was created. There's no reason to hold that against me, is there? Just because I'm a psychotic, armor-plated, Cthulhoid beast from beyond the pits of Hell, it doesn't mean we can't be friends. I like you humans as much as the next guy. It's not your fault that you all taste so incredibly delicious. Please come out. I'm only trying to be friendly. All I want is to say hello and then perhaps flay you alive, tear you apart and devour your innards with some crackers and a glass of Chianti. What's so wrong about that? There's nothing to be afraid of. Death comes naturally to all creatures. I'm just trying to advance the cycle. So what if I'm fifteen feet tall and have spikes all over my body, claws like scimitars, several barbed tails and a name the human tongue can't pronounce? That doesn't make me a bad person! I have feelings too, you know. Sure, maybe I'm planning to tear you limb from limb, taste some of those juicy internal organs of yours and play music with your bones, but it doesn't mean I'm insensitive! You will all be devoured sooner or later, and you must have a terribly busy schedule—I know I have. So, why not come out and at least get the screaming and dying part out of the way? It's only my job to rend you asunder, scatter your entrails about in an artistic fashion and smear tic-tac-toe symbols all over the walls with your spurting blood. It's not my fault if I enjoy it!

[MALEVOLENT LAUGHTER ENSUES]

WOOKIE LOVE

[A BASELINE PLAYS]

ANNOUNCER:

> And now, Mr. Barry White will read his new love poem, entitled
>
> **<title is spoken in Wookie language>**.

BARRY WHITE:

> Come on, baby, climb down from that tree.
> Be my co-pilot and we'll be flyin' free.
> Let me run my hands up and down your fur.
> I've got some lovin' that'll make you purr.
> Don't worry, baby, about bein' so tall.
> There's enough of you for us to do it all.
> I've been longing to hear your lovin' howl.
> As we sit among the stars like two night owls.
> Away put your weapon; set aside your bowcaster.
> I've got all the lovin' you'll need to last you.
> So let's go, baby; there's no need to bite,
> 'Cause we'll be makin' Wookie Love all through the night.

CRUISE CONTROL

Hey there, ladies and gentlemen! I hope you're all enjoying yourselves on this maiden voyage of the *Nosferatu*. We all seem to be having a swinging evening, and the fun's just started. We'll have the band play for you again in just a moment, but first, I've got a little announcement for you that the captain has just handed down to me. We want you to know that the bump you felt a minute ago did a negligible amount of damage. We are taking on a bit of water, but it's nothing to worry about. If you're wondering about that slight leaning you're feeling... yes, the ship is sinking, but there should be plenty of time to get everyone off. So, don't be alarmed—there's no need to panic. We'll escort you to the top deck when it's time. Just remember not to rush for the lifeboats. They're all big and comfy, so there'll be room for almost everyone. Don't be concerned about all the running around and siren wailing you're hearing. That's just the crew getting to their posts to give us a little more time before we capsize. Now, I see a few of you looking out the portholes, and yes, those are sharks out there, but they're friendly, so there's no need to worry. Just make sure they see you're having a good time and they'll leave you alone. If you look out to starboard, you'll see that there's an island just about three quarters of a mile away where we can wait until help arrives. And, yes, that volcano you see there is active, but most of the lava should be out of the way by the time we get there, and at least we won't have to send a flare up, right? Now, when you get up on deck, you'll each be handed a life preserver—just in case—and escorted to the lifeboats. Please put your preservers on right away. They're functional and stylish, too. When you get up there, don't be concerned if you happen to glimpse a long, serpentine creature to the port side of the ship—yes, it IS the thing that hit us, but don't worry. Our resident marine biologist says it was just looking for food. The lifeboats are all the way over on the starboard side, anyway, so as long as you row fast, there should be nothing to worry about. I know some of us could use the exercise, right? Well, they should be sending for us any minute now, but in the mean time, let the party continue! Now, let's hear the *Nosferatu* Jazz Ensemble playing... well, it looks like the band's gone, but there's still plenty of pate' and caviar left. I'll see you on the top deck, and remember: women, children and guys with microphones first, huh?

FISH CONDOM

SALMON:
> Hi! As a salmon, I have to do a lot of spawning. And I mean a *lot* of spawning. But one problem that I always run into when I'm swimming from one end of the river to the other is the issue of protection. You see, most regular condoms aren't made for aquatic life forms and tend to fall off or lose their effectiveness underwater. With the sheer amount of spawning I do every day, getting my protection to last for more than a few seconds can be nigh impossible. That is, until now! The newest rubber manufacturing technology has produced the most amazing invention ever known to ichthyologists. Gefilte Industries is proud to present its newest product: Pisces Condoms. Yes, Pisces Condoms have combined strong protection with the latest diving suit innovations to produce a prophylactic that's virtually unbreakable, waterproof and unbelievably comfortable! That can mean a lot to those of us that keep our reproductive organs inside. Pisces Condoms have all the extra strength I need to make it back to the spawning bed. But they're not just for salmon. There's a whole range of Pisces Condoms for fish of all kinds. They come extra-smooth for tuna when spawning on the run, and ribbed for halibuts that need that extra edge. There are special sound-dampening condoms for you lucky catfish, extra-wide condoms for manta rays, extra-light ones for jellyfish, and for you swordfish out there

they have specially reinforced prophylactics to help prevent puncture during fellatio. They even have extra-long life condoms for you sharks that are always on the move, and collapsible condoms for you sardines. Yes, Pisces Condoms bring aquatic lovemaking to a whole new level. Now, if they can only come up with a cigarette that'll light underwater, I'll be all set!

ANNOUNCER:

Pisces Condoms. Available at aquariums and bait stores everywhere. Get some today.

FORENSICS 101

Well class, today we're cutting straight to the meat of our course, if you'll excuse the pun, and diving right into our first autopsy. Now, I'm afraid that the morgue was out of fresh cadavers, so Mr. Stephens has volunteered to help us out. Bob, Grant, could you bring Mr. Stephens in, please? No, go ahead and unlock it. Good. Well, go in and get him. **(pause)** Ah, Mr. Stephens, thank you for joining us. No, let him go. Now... Now, please, there's no reason to get all excited, sir. Please, get down off the counter. There's no need to make it difficult. Please. No, please, put down the chair. It's Plexiglas anyway, you won't be able to... Now, now, Mr. Stephens, let's be sensible. Boys, if you would, please. Thank you. No, there's no reason to damage him. Bring him over here. Now really, such language. Now get up on the table please, sir. Come on. Just hop up onto the table. There's no need to be childish. Now, come on. Hop up. Jump up. Right here. Come on. Gentlemen, please... Now, do settle down, Mr. Stephens. Settle down. If you just hold still, we won't have to use the straps. **(sigh)** Very well, have it your way. Boys... Thank you. Now, class, gather around. Mr. Stephens will be playing the role of a poison victim and it's up to us to find some trace of it for identification. We'll start with an incision across the midsection, here. Not so loud, please, Mr. Stephens, I haven't even started yet! Now, you should make the first cut carefully, but precisely, like so... Oh, do stop screaming, sir. My goodness, there's quite a lot of blood in him, isn't there? Now, we make a second incision across the first one, like this. Ah. Yes, that's much better. Really throwing himself into the role now, isn't he? Let's proceed....

PHONE SEX

Thank you for calling the sex hotline.
If you want to hear deep moaning, press 1 now.
If you want to hear a girl talking dirty to ya, press 2.
If you want to hear some guy talking dirty to ya, press 3.
If you want to listen to some foreplay, press 4.
If you want to hear a realistic-sounding orgasm, press 5.
If you want to hear snoring, press 6.
To hear a string of profanity, press 7.
To hear the cops breaking in on a couple having sex, press 8.
If you just want to hear bed springs, press 9.
To repeat these choices, press the pound sign (for those of you without your GED, that's the little Tic-Tac-Toe symbol under the 9). And, if you're dialing from a rotary telephone, then you're out of luck, 'cause we ain't got the resources to have operators standing by around the clock just to breathe loud for your sorry ass.
Again, thanks for calling.

AUTO RACING SPECTATOR

How long do you think that doctor's been out there? Did you see the crash? The driver simply flew across the track and into the pit! Oh... He's getting up, I see. Still, that's what it's all about, eh? Those moments of suspense as a driver loses control and spins haphazardly into the stands, and no one knows whose soul will depart, and whose will stay! I love the Grand Prix. Ah, they're starting up again. Sometimes I wonder why they bother. These drivers look cadaverous enough as it is. So they can fit into tinier cars, I suppose. Oh, it's not like in the old days, when I'd come and watch. Huge, lovely, decorated cars... Huge, lovely, decorated wrecks. Ah, the pieces would fly everywhere when one of those babies ran into a wall or another car. I remember one time when a driver landed upside-down in a corner of the track. He was trapped—just wedged in there. There was such a stir among the crowd as all the emergency vehicles appeared. They had to use the jaws of life, in the end. Rather ironic, really, as he was beyond help. It took him hours to die, though! It was marvelous. Another time, a vehicle was catapulted into the stands, taking dozens of spectators up in one glorious second with a magnificent ball of flame. It was simply delicious! So many deaths in such a brief span of time! That's why this sport is so popular! It has incredible moments that are simply to die for, if you'll excuse the pun. When my time comes, I shall have a steering wheel mounted on my coffin to commemorate it. What... Wait... Ah, yes! Yes! Do you see that? Brilliant! No chance of survival there! If you'll excuse me, I shall have to get his measurements as soon as the smoke clears. I tell you, our little mortuary is just stacked to the gills this season!

VOODOO CLINIC

Ah, come in, sir. Your medical report says that you have persistent prostate trouble and that no other doctors have been able to help you. So now you have come to me. A wise choice. Here at the Voodoo Clinic, our methods are considered by many to be unusual but I assure you we are most thorough. Other doctors merely treat your problems with medicine, but we solve them once and for all by manipulating the spiritual forces that cause them in the first place. I shall do this for you, but you must have faith in the procedure or else the dark spirits that hold sway over your prostate will only tighten their grip. Have you brought a token for sacrifice? Good. Then remove your trousers and we shall begin.

> *I speak to those who seek in hunger*
> *To rend this man's prostate asunder.*
> *To cleave his manhood now in twain*
> *And bring him much enlarging pain.*
> *Demons, flee from out his member!*
> *Else be singed like burning embers!*
> *I call upon spirits of fire*
> *To burn away his penile ire!*
> *To bring his fluids back to stream!*
> *Be gone now evil, dark dick-fiends!*
> *I summon flames to burn their hate!*
> *To scorch the beasts from his prostate!*

It's all right, sir. We are finished. And as you can see, it is working already. Your wife will be very pleased by the rather vigorous side-effects. Now, do you have insurance? Excellent. You may go now and see the nurse in the waiting room on your way out. Be gone! I must meditate…. **(pause)** Viagara, eat your heart out.

PARANORMAL INSURANCE

Anyone who has to support a family has thought about what they'd do in case of floods, hurricanes and earthquakes, but have you ever considered the problems associated with hauntings and demonic possessions? If your house becomes infested with ghosts or wraiths, what will you do? If your basement floor suddenly breaks open and thousands of imps and goblins from the deepest pits of hell come pouring up out of the earth, you're going to need a good insurance company to help you through the aftermath of the crisis. Here at Metro Eternity, we understand that these things happen and we can provide coverage for a wide range of supernatural threats. Our insurance agents are well versed in the occult and can help you deal with anything from small problems like a rain of frogs in your back yard to major concerns like gargoyle or vampire attacks. They can also help you reduce the risk of bodily and property damage from poltergeists, zombies and other such entities by drawing arcane symbols in the parts of your house where you spend the most time and spraying your walls and most valuable possessions with holy water. We know how expensive a professional exorcist can be and we want to work with you to make sure your otherworldly problems are taken care of with a minimum of fuss. So remember, if a necromancer breaks into your house, summons the minions of Azathoth and lets them begin playing croquet with the skulls of your house pets on your patio, Metro Eternity is on your side.

ANTI-TALK SHOW

Tonight on Firing Line, we discuss the subject of coffee and try to answer the question: is there too much caffeine in it and what effect is it having on the US population? We have an expert here in the studio, Mr. Jorge Valdez. We'll be talking to him in a moment and we'll be taking some of your calls as well. The number is 555-9153. Jorge, I'd like to start by asking a simple question: do you think there's too much caffeine in the coffee? Now, before you answer that, let me show you these figures we got from the University of Virginia; according to this chart, there's been a geometric increase in the nation's caffeine levels over the last 30 years. Let's go to the phones for a reaction to that. Hello, LA! You're on the air. Hello? LA? Hello? Hello? Looks like we got cut off. We'll go to another call in a moment. But, if you're just tuning in, tonight, on Time Line, we discuss toffee: is there too much sugar in it and what effect is it having on the US population? Jorge, do you think the sugar content of toffee is having an adverse effect on the population? Take your time. Think about it. And in the mean time, let's take a look at these figures from the University of Cambridge. But first, let's take another call. Hello, Cleveland! You're on the air! Cleveland? Hello? You'll have to speak up, Cleveland, I can't hear you. Cleveland? We'll transfer you back to the operator and get this straightened out. The number is 555-3519. Tonight, on Party Line, we discuss rainwater: is it too wet? Jorge, how soggy did you get walking from the cab to the studio this evening? Take your time. Let's go to the phones. Hello, Madrid! You're on the air. Madrid? Hello? I'm sorry, Madrid, I can't understand you. Madrid? We'll transfer you back to the translator and get this straightened out. The number is 555-5391. Let's look at these figures from the University of Berlin. They're huge! Tonight, on Clothes Line, we discuss spaghetti: is it too stringy? Let's take a call. Hello, Geneva! You're on the air! Awesome, isn't it? Jorge, would you say that your last meal was stringy, very stringy or not stringy at all? Hang on, Jorge. Hello, Moscow! You're on the air! Before we take your question, Moscow, take a look at these figures from the University of Sydney. Aren't they pretty? The number is 555-6666. Tonight, on Conga Line, we discuss dance moves: are they getting too risky? Tell us, Jorge, how bad is the muscle pain you're getting from all those splits you do on the dance floor every night? Hello, Johannesburg! You're on the air! The number is 555-6969. Jorge, any final comments? I'm sorry, we're out of time. Next time, on Streamline, we'll answer the question: is there too much crack in my coffee?! Goodnight!

THIS IS THE END

Good evening, and welcome to World News Nightly. I'm the late James Ryan. Our top story tonight: the world has come to an end. In a surprise turn of events the world ended last night on New Year's Eve after an accident with a large particle accelerator in Switzerland. It is believed the accident took place during the research facility's New Year's Eve party. The common perception had been that the world was not scheduled to end until December 21st, 2012, but it has been pointed out that since Armageddon has come and there are no more calendars, it doesn't really matter any more. God could not be reached for comment, but Her press secretary has released the following statement: "The next Earth will be even more spectacular than the last model, and this time, we respectfully recommend that you not build any more particle accelerators. Public services will be resumed as soon as possible. Thank you." In other news… nothing. There is absolutely nothing happening anywhere on Earth. This is most likely due to the fact that the world had ended. We have some closings for you. Well, it looks like all schools and businesses will be closed until further notice except for technical and community colleges, which will be under a two-hour delay. In sports, Honolulu beat Dallas 7 to nothing in the last game, and they were to be going on to the playoffs later this month, only now they can't. According to the latest weather report, IT'S RAINING FROGS! IT'S RAINING FROGS! IT'S RAINING FROGS! Apparently, it's still raining frogs. We expect this condition to last… for a very long time. Well, that's the news for this evening, so until the next life, this is the late James Ryan saying good night and I'll see you on the other side.